SNARE DRUM PLAY-ALONG

MELODIC RUDIMENTS WITH BACKING TRACKS IN ALL STYLES

by Joe Cox

ISBN 978-1-4234-8726-5

HAL•LEONARD®
CORPORATION

7777 W. BLUEMOUND RD. P.O. BOX 13819 MILWAUKEE, WI 53213

In Australia Contact:
Hal Leonard Australia Pty. Ltd.
4 Lentara Court
Cheltenham, Victoria, 3192 Australia
Email: ausadmin@halleonard.com.au

Visit Hal Leonard Online at
www.halleonard.com

contents

INTRODUCTION

Learning the "Standard 26 American Drum Rudiments" is essential for every drummer. But just practicing with a pad or a snare drum, speeding up then slowing down in the traditional method, can become a bit tedious.

This book has been designed to help intermediate and advanced drummers develop rudiment speed with play-along tracks that start slowly, accelerate, then slow back down. But what sets it apart from other rudiment books is musical grooves, in a number of different styles, that help the drummer hear the sticking patterns. The melodies in the tracks mirror and/or complement the left and right hands of the rudiment.

The first 26 tracks of the CD have progressive tempos that move from moderately slow to *usefully* fast, then slow back down at the end. Tracks 27 through 52 maintain a moderate practice tempo for about a minute.

This book and the accompanying play-alongs will motivate any drummer to work longer and get better at rudiments because they make practice fun!

SINGLE STROKE ROLL

Track 1 Progressive Tempo ♩ = 80–170–80
Track 27 Practice Tempo

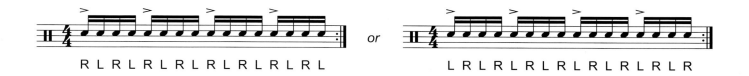

R L R L R L R L R L R L R L R L   or   L R L R L R L R L R L R L R L R

 The single stroke roll is usually one of the first fills a drummer learns. It's, of course, pretty easy to execute.

> **TIP** Pay attention to your stick height, making all the strokes look the same. Accents have been added just because in popular music it would be unusual to play single strokes without *some* kind of accent. You can start with the accent in your dominant hand. But, learn to play the rudiment with the accents in either stick. Don't get in the habit of always favoring your dominant hand.

If you find the progressive tempo of the track to be too easy, you can experiment with accents on different strokes.

At the slower tempo, you can play with ALL WRIST, with a pretty good grip on the sticks. As the tempo accelerates, you can start to free the sticks and use bounce.

Another way to practice with the track is to play eighth-note singles with each hand separately. It's fun to alternate between measures, playing 8 strokes per measure.

Preparatory Exercise:

R   R   R   R   R   R   R   R   L   L   L   L   L   L   L   L

If you have trouble making it to the fastest place in the track, go to track 27 and practice the rudiment at a moderate tempo.

DOUBLE STROKE OPEN ROLL

Track 2 Progressive Tempo ♩ = 66–170–66
Track 28 Practice Tempo

```
R R L L R R L L R R L L R R L L   R R L L R R L L R R L L R R L L
```

Follow the ascending melody with alternating right and left sticks. You can actually start just by playing the eighth notes in preparation for the rudiment. When you are comfortable with the eighth notes, just add the double in every stroke.

Preparatory Exercise:

```
R   L   R   L   R   L   R   L     R   L   R   L   R   L   R   L
```

It is important to play the strokes very evenly. This is why the track sounds somewhat mechanical. You should have machine precision in your strokes.

As the track accelerates, it is important to get a lift of the sticks, so that your strokes don't become buzzes. You should hear every sixteenth note.

 If you are using the bounce technique, the tips of your sticks should be hovering around 24 inches above your pad or the drumhead. This is an exaggerated motion, but it will help you get more lift on the sticks, resulting in a clean execution. Your wrists should be moving with the eighth notes.

As you get into the groove of the double stroke and the speed increases, you can add accents like this:

```
R R L L R R L L R R L L R R L L
```

Go to track 28 if you need to practice at a steady tempo.

FIVE STROKE ROLL

Track 3 Progressive Tempo ♩ = 75–165–75
Track 29 Practice Tempo

Woodblocks

R R L L R   L L R R L   R R L L R   L L R R L

ow you'll start hearing pitches on the track, which will help your sticking pattern. A higher pitch represents the right stick and a lower pitch represents the left stick. It's as though you were sitting in front of a keyboard, playing the rudiment with right hand higher and left lower. Although the pitches will be different in the various tracks, this high-low convention is kept throughout.

In this track, two woodblocks guide your sticking pattern.

Do not overlook the accents. Concentrate on symmetry between the right and the left accents. Listen to yourself as you play. The accents should sound the same. The placement of the accents is enhanced on the track by a finger cymbal.

Accents should be executed with a "downstroke" motion. The accenting stick is raised higher for a solid stroke, the wrist is snapped, and as soon as the surface is struck, the stick is gripped a little tighter and "freezes" over the playing surface about 2 inches.

The focus of all these exercises is musical interpretation of the 26 rudiments and to provide a platform for practicing. Your instructor can give you a more detailed description of stick control and help you with technical nuances.

Think of the five stroke roll as "2 + 1," meaning 2 doubles and a single.

To practice the five stroke roll at a moderate tempo without acceleration, go to track 29.

If you're a five stroke monster, you might try playing to track 3 in double time. You may fold before you get to the maximum speed, but it's fun trying:

R R L L **R** L L R R **L**   R R L L **R** L L R R **L**

SEVEN STROKE ROLL

Track 4 Progressive Tempo ♩ = 100–160–100
Track 30 Practice Tempo

RRLLRRLRRLLRRL RRLLRRLRRLLRRL LLRRLLRLLRRLLR LLRRLLRLLRRLLR

Think of the seven stroke roll as "3 + 1" - 3 doubles plus a single stroke. You can use the preparatory practice exercise to feel this 3 + 1.

Preparatory Exercise:

R L R L **R** L R L R L R L **R** L R L L R L **R** L R L **R** L R L **R** L R L **R**

The left stick accent is enhanced by a D and the right accent by the note a fifth higher, the A.

As in all the double stroke roll rudiments, the accents are critical. Play these accents in the same way you played the five stroke roll.

Don't forget to listen to your rudiment as you play it. Are your accents sounding alike in both sticks? They should be.

 This would be a good time to remind you to not be lazy and just play the rudiment with your dominant hand. Sometimes drummers mistakenly think that those second underlying stickings on the rudiment charts are optional. No, every rudiment should be played with equal fluidity on both sides.

This is also a good time to make the simple observation that practicing rudiments is not supposed to be an arduous task and an end unto itself. All the rudiments are musical. When you move to your kit, you will find little pieces of or entire rudiments moving into your playing. Fill ideas will come to you, and you'll play them more easily with more confidence.

Track 30 is the moderate, constant tempo version.

nine stroke roll

Track 5 Progressive Tempo ♩ = 90–180–90
Track 31 Practice Tempo

(2-bar prep on CD)

R R L L R R L L R L L R R L L R R L R R L L R R L L R L L R R L L R R L

In this track you will hear the melodic notes which correspond to your right and left hands. Hopefully listening to these two notes on the track will help your nine stroke roll. In other words, every time you hear those pitches, your right or left wrist should be moving in the downward direction.

If you need the preparatory exercise, play it with NO bounce, all wrist, and a fairly firm stick grip. When you are comfortable with that wrist motion, you can free up the sticks to bounce twice to every wrist motion. It's a rhythmic bounce. Let the sticks do the work. You don't have to MAKE the sticks execute the double. If your wrists are moving with the melody, the sticks will practically play themselves.

Preparatory Exercise:

R L R L **R** L R L R **L** R L R L **R** L R L R **L**

So let's talk about your shoulders. They should be relaxed. If you are sitting in front of the practice pad or snare drum, sit up straight. Relax your elbows as well. Don't let your elbows start to rise away from your sides. You don't need to FORCE the elbows into your body, but just let them hang naturally. Let your hands be relaxed, especially when you are bouncing your doubles. Finally, don't clinch your jaw or let your tongue become rigid. This may sound silly, but if you tense up as the track increases in tempo, your jaw and tongue will turn to stone.

Sometimes students drop their sticks. But that's okay. It just means that they are relaxed. A death grip from your shoulders to your fingers is the WORSE thing you can do for your playing.

ten stroke roll

Track 6 Progressive Tempo ♩ = 100–180–100
Track 32 Practice Tempo

RRLLRRLLR L   RRLLRRLLR L   LLRRLLRRL R   LLRRLLRRL R

The ten stroke roll is a rather aggressive rudiment that's really fun to play.

Throw away those first four doubles. It's the ACCENTS you're going for. Play those accents with tons of intention. As each stick comes down for the accent, it freezes a couple of inches above the playing surface. This means that at the end of those two bold accents, BOTH sticks should hover at the same height. Think of this as a "stop motion." Just for a second, everything comes to a hard, rhythmic pause. Then the sticks drop for the doubles again.

You can also experiment with adding a crescendo over beats 1 and 3. This will give the rudiment an extra musical dynamic.

Just be aware of the symmetry of your sticking. And have fun with the accents!

As the track slows down again, relax and follow it. Don't get ahead. (It's tempting to rush!)

Preparatory Exercise:

R L R L **R L**   R L R L **R L**   L R L R **L R**   L R L R **L R**

ELEVEN STROKE ROLL

Track 7 Progressive Tempo ♩ = 80–160–80
Track 33 Practice Tempo

RRLLRRLLRRL   RRLLRRLLRRL   LLRRLLRRLLR   LLRRLLRRLLR

Follow the lead sax in the track.

A note about the rhythmic notation of the rudiments in this book: each rudiment follows the rhythmic scan of *The Standard 26 American Drum Rudiments* as published by the Percussive Arts Society. Whether eighths or sixteenths were used in the notation depended on the feel of the track.

Slashes on the stems of drum notes are often confusing, especially when trying to show how the sticking works with each rudiment. In these exercises, you see every note, so there is no doubt about how the sticking is executed. Sometimes arrangers will throw in those slash marks, somewhat unsure of their true intention.

Another reason for using different rhythmic notations: ALL these rudiments have real-world application and need to be understood in a musical context, not just as stand-alone exercises.

Students also get confused just by the name of a rudiment: "eleven stroke roll" or "fifteen stroke roll." What's up with that? Why should I learn those? The eleven stroke roll as you see it here is very musical and makes a nice fill in the fourth bar of the phrase.

THIRTEEN STROKE ROLL

Track 8 Progressive Tempo ♩ = 80–160–80
Track 34 Practice Tempo

R R L L R R L L R R L L R   L L R R L L R R L L R R L

In the classic rudiment, shown above, the thirteenth stroke is the accented note. You should really give this stroke a solid swing of the wrist.

Another variation is to add accents to every beat, which fits the feel of the track very well:

R R L L **R** R L L **R** R L L **R**   **L** L R R **L** L R R **L** L R R **L**

Still another variation will help your dynamic control:

R R L L R R L L R R L L **R**   L L R R L L R R L L R R **L**
mp ——————————*f*   *mp* ——————————*f*

 This is a good time to remind you to play in the center of your snare drum or pad with your sticks at that sweet 90-degree angle. (Remember not to stick out your elbows!)

Track 9 Progressive Tempo ♩ = 90–160–90
Track 35 Practice Tempo

R R L L R R L L R R L L R R L   R R L L R R L L R R L L R R L

L L R R L L R R L L R R L L R   L L R R L L R R L L R R L L R

These eighth notes below are the motion of the wrist if you are bouncing the sixteenth note doubles:

Preparatory Exercise:

R L R L R L R L   R L R L R L R L   L R L R L R L R   L R L R L R L R

If you really want to have fun with the accent, take a really exaggerated swing. The tip of the stick will go over the shoulder and the action is a whipping motion with a snap of the wrist.

Students sometimes are intimidated by the fifteen stroke roll. Just the NAME kind of gets overwhelming. And they wonder why anyone should ever bother with such a rudiment. (Good thing the seventeen stroke roll is not included in the "Standard 26"!) But don't give up if you find it difficult. Just think 7+1 (7 doubles and a single). If it helps, count the 7 doubles out loud.

In this book we're into real-world application of the rudiments, especially as they are used in your kit playing. And this one makes a great fill, which you hear in the track every fourth bar. Listen for the crash cymbal on the eighth-note accent.

SINGLE PARADIDDLE

Track 10 Progressive Tempo ♩ = 55–140–55
Track 36 Practice Tempo

R L R R L R L L R L R R L R L L   R L R R L R L L R L R R L R L L

The single paradiddle is probably THE most popular rudiment. Even an adult who played a drum in grade school band but hasn't played since probably still remembers the paradiddle.

It's one of those rudiments that is named for how it sounds, which also makes it easy to remember. It's also a very cool-sounding rudiment and gets cooler the faster you play it. The applications on the kit are endless. And it's a fabulous exercise for double bass.

Preparatory Exercise:

R R R **L** L L **R** R R **L** L L   **R** R R **L** L L **R** R R **L** L L

If you've been playing a while, and the paradiddle comes naturally to you, move the accent over to the second sixteenth of each beat. Then the third, then the fourth. That will make the paradiddle much more challenging. (Warning: the last one is brutal, even for the most experienced "paradiddler.")

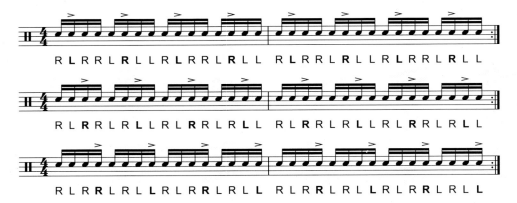

R L **R** R L R L L R L **R** R L R L L   R L **R** R L R L L R L **R** R L R L L

R L R **R** L R L L R L R **R** L R L L   R L R **R** L R L L R L R **R** L R L L

R L R R **L** R L L R L R R **L** R L L   R L R R **L** R L L R L R R **L** R L L

Have fun and invent your own accent variations. Use track 36 for experimenting with accents and dynamics.

DOUBLE PARADIDDLE

Track 11 Progressive Tempo ♩ = 88–178–88
Track 37 Practice Tempo

(2-bar prep on CD)

RLRLRRLRLRLL RLRLRRLRLRLL RLRLRR LRLRLL RLRLRR LRLRLL

The double paradiddle is often presented in 6/8 time. But in this track it is in 4/4 with a triplet feel. Try to lock in to the bass line.

You will do this groove very well if you really feel the first- and third-beat accents. This is one where you can get your whole upper body into the motion, even your head, which can swing or rotate from side to side.

Preparatory Exercise:

RLRL LRLR RLRL LRLR RLRL LRLR RLRL LRLR

This rudiment really is ALL about the accent. The triplets, except for the accents, are small. The ratio of accents to the rest of the notes is 100 to 10. Or you might think of the triplets following the main accents as ghost notes. They are hardly there. With this kind of feel, your double paradiddle will be very musical and satisfying.

If you're having trouble with a rudiment, put your sticks down. Place your hands on your knees. Practice the rudiment with your hands, but keep the wrist connected with the top of your leg. You can practice like this anytime—in class, at work, on a break, or while watching TV. When you put sticks in your hands to play the rudiment, they are like a natural extension of that up and down wrist motion with your hands.

FLAM

Track 12 Progressive Tempo ♩ = 78–158–78
Track 38 Practice Tempo

LR   RL   LR   RL   LR   RL   LR   RL

Picture a mechanical toy monkey with a drum. Or a toy soldier playing a marching drum. This is the way your hands and sticks should look as you play the flam! Not only that, but you should be just as machine-like and precise in your movements.

 It takes practice to get the grace note to have just the right feel: too close to the main stroke and it sounds like a double hit or a recorded snare drum out of phase (technically called a flat flam); too wide, and it becomes something else altogether, like a sixteenth note.

The flam is just a way of adding character or thickness to a single stroke. A flam can make a backbeat sound huge.

If you need more challenge playing the flam, you can play in double time and start with eighths. Good luck making it all the way to the top speed of the track. It IS fun to try it.

The placement of the hands before the stroke is very important! Right stick up, left stick about 2 inches above the head.

After the first stroke, the hands have essentially traded places.

FLAM ACCENT

Track 13 Progressive Tempo ♩. = 56–126–56
Track 39 Practice Tempo

(2-bar prep on CD)

LR L RrL R L LR L RrL R L LR L RrL R L LR L RrL R L

LR L RrL R L LR L RrL R L LR L RrL R L LR L RrL R L

This is another rudiment which is named for how it sounds, so it is easy to remember. It has not just a triplet feel, but a SUPER triplet feel. It just rides along, defining what a triplet means.

 Get your sticks in the air for the accent. Then let the rest of the strokes hover about 3 or 4 inches away from your playing surface.

This rudiment can be the seed of a great fill in blues or shuffle tunes.

Just lay back with the track. This rudiment has a great groove, so just relax.

The tempo of the loop goes as far as it can before starting to sound cartoonish. But, of course, you may be able to perform this rudiment even faster. If you can set your metronome to a dotted quarter equals 176 and play that for a minute, you're doing great. Perhaps you can play it even faster. If so, go for it!

Crazy, blistering speed and feats of athleticism are NOT what we're going for in this set of rudiments and tracks. Musical application is the point. Build your speed gradually and enjoy the process.

Preparatory Exercise:

LR R RrL L LR R RrL L LR R RrL L LR R RrL L

FLam tap

Track 14 Progressive Tempo ♩ = 80–160–80
Track 40 Practice Tempo

(2-bar prep on CD)

LR RrL LLR RrL L LR RrL LLR RrL L LR RrL LLR RrL L LR RrL LLR RrL L

The siren-like sound is meant to help you keep your right and left strokes even.

The "tap" is just a rhythmic drop – it is a bounce or rebound from the accented stroke. Just a light tap. It's kind of like if you were just playing a flam, but were so loose with your sticks that another note crept in between the flams.

There is not a track for it, but here's another useful version of the flam tap, where you swing the eighths:

LR R rL L LR R rL L LR R rL L LR R rL L

Some drummers find the flam tap easier when they swing the eighths.

Either way, it's a fun rudiment. On your drum kit, play the right stick with the hi-hat and the left with the snare drum. Or try it as a fill with your sticks on two toms.

FLAMACUE

LR L R L LR   LR L R L LR   RL R L R RL   RL R L R RL

 or the accent, follow the accented snare drum on the track.

> **TIP** At the slower speed, there's a great big space in beats 2 and 4. So, play that space with intention and don't rush it. And where should your sticks be during that hole in the pocket? About 3 to 4 inches above the playing surface.

Here's the rudiment "naked," stripped of what makes it cool:

Preparatory Exercise:

R L R L R   R L R L R   L R L R L   L R L R L

Now put in the accent:

R L R L R   R L R L R   L R L R L   L R L R L

The rudiment grooves a little more with an accent on 2 and 4. Go to your kit and add the kick:

LR L R LLR   LR L R LLR   RL R L RRL   RL R L RRL

FLAM PARADIDDLE

Track 16 Progressive Tempo ♩ = 60–110–60
Track 42 Practice Tempo

L R L R R rL R L L L L R L R R rL R L L L R L R R rL R L L L L R L R R rL R L L

To help with sticking symmetry, listen for the higher and lower pitches. The accented stroke on the right stick matches up with the higher pitch. The accented stroke on the left stick matches up with lower pitches. If you are left-handed, you can reverse this. What's important is the alternating stick pattern. You can also hear a small hand drum playing the "diddle."

 If your rudiment breaks down before you get to the fastest tempo on the track, don't worry. Most of the rudiments take a lot of practice. We measure progress in rudiments by how fast and precisely we can play them. If you get confused and your sticks go into a jumble, you can either stop and wait for the track to begin to slow down OR you can just start over.

What you DON'T want to do is continue to attempt to play faster if your strokes are not clean and things are getting sloppy, like doubles sounding more like buzzes, or leaving out doubles altogether.

Don't cheat on your sticking. Sometimes it's really easy to do. That's where a good teacher can help by watching and listening to your playing, correcting if your rudiment is not quite right.

The flam paradiddle sounds very cool with the left hand on a higher tom and the right on a lower one. Try it. And make up your own combinations.

FLAM PARADIDDLE-DIDDLE

Track 17 Progressive Tempo ♪ = 96–200–96
Track 43 Practice Tempo

L R L R R L L L R L R L L R R   L R L R R L L L R L R L L R R

Hey diddle-diddle. Baby, ooh yeah!

The track has a laid-back feel, with emphasis on that backbeat accent.

This is one of the most difficult rudiments.

It's interesting that, in the single paradiddle-diddle, which is not included in the "Standard 26," you're allowed to repeat the accented stick two or even four times before switching the pattern:

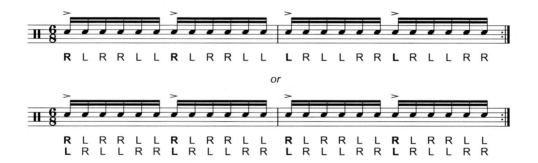

R L R R L L R L R R L L   L R L L R R L R L L R R

or

R L R R L L R L R R L L   R L R R L L R L R R L L
L R L L R R L R L L R R   L R L L R R L R L L R R

That doesn't seem fair, does it? The single diddle-diddle is much easier.

So, for that reason, as a preparatory exercise, leave out the flam to get the feel of the sticking. Once you're comfortable, you can add the flams, which add character and pizzazz to the rudiment.

If you're learning the flam paradiddle-diddle for the first time, you should practice it a LOT with hands on knees.

Count out loud. Pat your right or left foot on the floor with the accents. Or use the kick or the hat. With practice, you'll be doing some great stuff with this rudiment!

L R L R R L L L R L R L L R R   L R L R R L L L R L R L L R R

DRAG

(4-beat prep on CD)

LL R   RR L   LL R   RR L   LL R   RR L   LL R   RR L   LL R

RR L   LL R   RR L   LL R   RR L   LL R   RR L

The drag seems so easy, but it is really not. It is not two sixteenths followed by an eighth. The speed at which you play the drag is determined by tempo. The drag is there to add "character" to the main stroke. The drag is two grace notes that are played according to what "feels right." It will vary, depending on the musical situation.

TIP

The stick mechanics are very much like those used in the flam. Remember that the sound of the sticks should be the same from left to right. When you begin, the right stick is raised almost to a vertical position and the left stick is 2 to 3 inches from the playing surface. After the left stick plays the two grace notes, it flies up to the vertical position and the sticks have switched position. Observe all these details and your drags will sound great!

Welcome to Hollywood.
Click tracks.
The clock is ticking.
Perfect reading.
Perfect takes.
No second chances.
Time signatures that change every measure.

PERCUSSION

TITANS
#27A

♩ = 130
SNARE

SINGLE DRAG TAP

Track 19 Progressive Tempo ♩ = 70–120–70
Track 45 Practice Tempo

LLR L RRL R LLR L RRL R LLR L RRL R LLR L RRL R

A note about the track styles on the CD: a professional drummer should be proficient in many styles of music. It is fun to play rudiments to a variety of genres.

For this track and rudiment, even if you don't particularly care for the style, go ahead and work with the track. Lay back and just have some fun. Even serious metal players have been known to smile while playing with this country track.

 Think of the accent velocity as 100 percent, with the other strokes being around 20 percent. Your hands should be loose and easy.

If you're playing the single drag tap perfectly, and you can't stand any more slide steel guitar, here's a double bass exercise for you:

And if that's still not enough for you, try this: (If you can play this example, you are a metal machine!)

Make up your own applications for the single drag tap. Using various combinations of toms, it makes a nice fill-in for straight-eighth rock. Just be sure to keep the accents equally balanced.

DOUBLE DRAG TAP

Track 20 Progressive Tempo ♪ = 112–208–108
Track 46 Practice Tempo

In execution and form, the double drag tap is like the single drag tap. To help guide you from the left to the right accent, listen to the saxophone staccato notes on the track. These hits should sync right with your accent.

This exercise will help you get a feel for the stick pattern:

Preparatory Exercise:

 The accent is a solid downstroke with a slight squeeze on the stick, preventing a rebound. If the accent stick flew back up, the stick would have too far to return for the next two strokes and the rudiment would sound choppy. Instead, as soon as you've made the downstroke and quick "freeze" motion, you drop the stick for the following two strokes.

Enough momentum is created by the accented downstroke so that the following strokes just fall easily.

Your drags should be pretty close to the playing surface, no more than 2 to 3 inches high. This happens by freezing the accented stroke at about that height.

LESSON 25

Track 21 Progressive Tempo ♪ = 100–200–100
Track 47 Practice Tempo

(8-beat prep on CD)

LLR L RLLR L RRrL R LrrL R L   LLR L RLLR L RRrL R LrrL R L

Lesson 25 has always been popular with students. It's a great rudiment that's cool to play and has lots of real music-world applications. When you play along with the track, listen for the two-sixteenths-plus-eighth pattern that's written for you above the rudiment.

To break down this rudiment, remove the drag and the sixteenth notes, reducing the rudiment to its most basic sticking pattern:

Preparatory Exercise:

R R R R L L L L R R R R L L L L

Now add the drag:

LLR RLLR RRrL LrrL L   LLR RLLR RRrL LrrL L

The above exercise should remind you of another rudiment: the single drag tap. Except now the accent follows on the same stick.

Finally, insert the sixteenth strokes and you've got it!

25

DR♭P R DiDDL #1

Track 22 Progressive Tempo ♪ = 120–208–120
Track 48 Practice Tempo

(2-bar prep on CD)

R LLR L R R L RRL R L L   R LLR L R R L RRL R L L

(Fill Bar)

R LLR L R R L RRL R L L   R LLR L R R L RRL R L L

You've GOT to be able to FEEL this rudiment. If you play it flat, (as it is unfortunately often presented in print or on internet videos) you'll never find it interesting and you'll never use it. It should sound bluesy. So, the track has a laid-back R&B feel. In the fourth bar of the loop, you'll hear the rudiment used as a fill on the kit.

 Get the groove down in your sticks. Then sing along with the track. No kidding. Sing along with the brass melody.

Next, show this rudiment to a friend, perhaps another musician. See if you can communicate the hip feel of this rudiment. See if you can draw your friend into the rhythm.

Don't play any of these rudiments like a machine! Play rudiments as pieces of music. Play expressively. Play with dynamics. Play with cool accents.

Finally, make up your own 4-bar melody (keeping the triplet feel) that you can sing over your rudiment. Experiment and have fun with it!

DRAG PARADIDDLE #2

Track 23 Progressive Tempo ♪ = 132–208–132
Track 49 Practice Tempo

R L L R L L R   L   R   R   L rr L rr L   R   L   L   R L L R L L R   L   R   R   L rr L rr L   R   L   L

When you're first learning a rudiment, you might have to keep your eyes glued to the page, paying a lot of attention to the sticking details.

But as the rudiment accelerates and it starts to feel natural, you should move your eyes away from the page. You can watch your sticks, being aware of symmetry between left and right strokes. Close your eyes and listen. Are you locking in with the track perfectly?

These practices will help you internalize the rudiments so that they become an integrated part of your musical and rhythmic vocabulary.

This exercise will help you hear and feel the major sticking changes. Listen to the piano lick, which guides you from right to left:

Preparatory Exercise:

R   R   R   R R L   L   L   L L   R   R   R   R R L   L   L   L L

Try this fill, starting with your right stick on a tom and your left stick on the snare:

R   L L R   L L R   L   R   R   L   rr L   rr L   R   L   L

SINGLE RATAMACUE

Track 24 Progressive Tempo ♩ = 100–160–100
Track 50 Practice Tempo

(2-bar prep on CD)

LLR L R L RRL R L R   LLR L R L RRL R L R

LLR L R L RRL R L R   LLR L R L RRL R L R

Whenever you practice a rudiment, whether you are working with one of these tracks, with a metronome, or just freehand, you should play for at least a minute.

> **TIP** Use a simple kitchen timer or an online countdown timer on your computer. There are many stopwatch programs on the internet. As a modern musician, you've got lots of tools available for assisting you in your practice. Use them!

If you've ever set a timer for a minute to practice a rudiment, you know that sometimes that minute takes forever. But sustaining a rudiment for a minute or longer commits it to muscle memory.

Preparatory Exercise:

RLRL LRLR RLRL LRLR RLRL LRLR RLRL LRLR

DOUBLE Ratamacue

Track 25 Progressive Tempo ♩ = 80–160–80
Track 51 Practice Tempo

LLR LLR L R L   RRL RRL R L R   LLR LLR L R L   RRL RRL R L R

The sax is playing a riff that follows the double ratamacue.

As in all the rudiments, don't forget the accent!

We don't learn rudiments so that when we're playing with a group we're thinking, "Ok, at the end of the verse I'll use a flam accent. And a single ratamacue works great at the bridge." Yes, a lot of rudiments make great fills just on their own. But that's not the point. The point of practicing rudiments is that your hands and sticks learn to work in so many different ways that when you're playing music, you'll hear ideas that you can execute with ease.

Your hands and sticks (and feet) serve your musical ideas and intuitions.

TRIPLE RATAMACUE

Track 26 Progressive Tempo ♩ = 100–170–100
Track 52 Practice Tempo

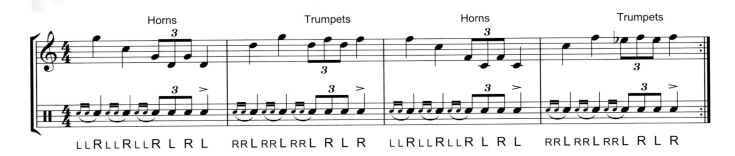

In review, here are ten very important concepts to keep in mind while practicing your rudiments:

1. **Always LISTEN as you play.** Do your strokes sound even?

2. **Don't forget to play the ACCENTS that are included in most rudiments.** They make rudiments groove.

3. **If you are using MATCHED grip, be sure the left and right hands and stick look matched.** You should have symmetry and balance between both sides.

4. **RELAX.** The faster you play, the more relaxed you need to be. Drop your shoulders and your elbows. Let your wrists be free and hold your sticks with a natural grip that is not too tight.

5. **Think about rudiments, even when you don't have sticks in your hand and a drum in front of you.** Practice with hands on knees or on a table. Load the CD tracks on to your portable player and you're ready to practice ANYWHERE!

6. **Learn and practice ALL the rudiments.** Don't get stuck in just your favorites.

7. **Practice any given rudiment for at LEAST a minute.** Practice five or six rudiments a day, at the same time, in the same place, with the same sticks. And stay focused.

8. **Don't cheat on the sticking.** Start by playing the rudiment as slow as necessary. When playing with one of the tracks, go as fast as you can while still being accurate. If you fold, wait until the track starts to slow down again and pick it up to the end. Try again tomorrow.

9. **EXPERIMENT with ways to incorporate rudiments into playing your kit.**

10. **Have FUN, even when you're practicing a difficult rudiment.**

the 26 Standard Rudiments

Single Stroke Roll

R L R L R L R L R L R L R L R L   R L R L R L R L R L R L R L R L

Double Stroke Open Roll

R R L L R R L L R R L L R R L L   R R L L R R L L R R L L R R L L

Five Stroke Roll

R R L L R L L R R L   R R L L R L L R R L

Seven Stroke Roll

R R L L R R L R R L L R R L   R R L L R R L R R L L R R L
L L R R L L R L L R R L L R   L L R R L L R L L R R L L R

Nine Stroke Roll

R R L L R R L L R   L L R R L L R R L

Ten Stroke Roll

R R L L R R L L R L   R R L L R R L L R L
L L R R L L R R L R   L L R R L L R R L R

Eleven Stroke Roll

R R L L R R L L R R L   R R L L R R L L R R L

Thirteen Stroke Roll

R R L L R R L L R R L R   L L R R L L R R L L R R L

Fifteen Stroke Roll

R R L L R R L L R R L L R R L   R R L L R R L L R R L L R R L
L L R R L L R R L L R R L L R   L L R R L L R R L L R R L L R

Single Paradiddle

R L R R L R L L R L R R L R L L   R L R R L R L L R L R R L R L L

Double Paradiddle

R L R L R R L R L R L L   R L R L R R L R L R L L

Flam

L R   R L   L R   R L   L R   R L   L R   R L

Flam Accent

L R L R R L R L   L R L R R L R L

Flam Tap

L R R R L L L R R R L L   L R R R L L L R R R L L

Flamacue

L R L R L L R L R L R L L R   R L R L R R L R L R L R R L

Lesson 25

L L R L R L L R L R L R R R L R L R R L R L   L L R L R L L L R L R L R R R L R L R R L R L

Flam Paradiddle

L R L R R R L R L L L R L R R R L R L L   L R L R R R L R L L L R L R R R L R L L

Drag Paradiddle #1

R L L R L R R L R R L R L L   R L L R L R R L R R L R L L

Flam Paradiddle-Diddle

L R L R R L L L R L R L L R R   L R L R R L L L R L R L L R R

Drag Paradiddle #2

R L L R L L R L R R L R R L R R L R L R   R L L R L L R L R R L R R L R R L R L L

Drag

L L R   R R L   L L R   R R L   L L R   R R L   L L R   R R L

Single Ratamacue

L L R L R L R R L R L R   L L R L R L R R L R L R

Single Drag Tap

L L R L R R L R L L R L R R L R   L L R L R R L R L L R L R R L R

Double Ratamacue

L L R   L L R   L R L   R R L   R R L   R L R

Double Drag Tap

L L R L L R   L R R L R R L   R   L L R L L R   L R R L R R L   R

Triple Ratamacue

L L R L L R L L R L R L   R R L R R L R R L R L R